CONTENTS

Series editor: Tim Carr

BIBLE SOCIETY
Stonehill Green, Westlea, SWINDON SN5 7DG, England

First published 1990

British Library Cataloguing in Publication Data
Hiscox, Rhoda
   Women in the church.
   1. Christian church. Role of women
   I. Title   II. Bible Society
   262'.15

ISBN 0–564–01504–0

Printed in Great Britain

Typeset in Times 11/13pt.

Bible Societies exist to provide resources for Bible distribution and use. Bible Society in England and Wales (BFBS) is a member of the United Bible Societies, an international partnership working in over 180 countries. Their common aim is to reach all people with the Bible, or some part of it, in a language they can understand and at a price they can afford. Parts of the Bible have now been translated into approximately 1900 languages. Bible Societies aim to help every church at every point where it uses the Bible. You are invited to share in this work by your prayers and gifts. The Bible Society in your country will be very happy to provide details of its activity.

HOW TO USE THIS BOOK

The six sessions follow a similar pattern.

TO BEGIN

Usually helps you to focus on some aspect of women's experience, either in general or in the Church. Incidentally, group leaders are advised, as part of their preparation, always to look through the following study as well in case there is any special preparation the group itself needs to make for the following session.

BIBLE

The main passages are printed in full but you will need to have Bibles with you to look up references from time to time. Reading the portion aloud with a narrator and group members taking the parts of the speakers helps to bring the Gospels to life and is more fun.

DIGGING DEEPER

Involves the challenge of letting the Bible speak to us, perhaps in unaccustomed ways. It may include some background information to help you understand the story. It encourages you to "dig deeper" and enter into the experience and meaning of the story for those who were there. Sometimes this means standing back from the story; at other times trying to stand in the shoes of the people who were present. It is not always easy to do this, but groups brave enough to try are often surprised at the ways in which their faith and insight begin to grow.

TO TALK ABOUT

Provides opportunities for the interplay of the good news of Jesus and your own experience. You are invited to share your thoughts and to think about the meaning of the story for your group. There will probably be too many questions to deal with at one meeting, so choose ones most suited to your group. You can always continue your thinking at home. Make sure your choices give people a chance to disagree!

TO PRAY

At the end of each session there are suggestions for prayer. If they are helpful use them, if not, pray together in ways which are helpful to your group. Don't be afraid to try new forms of prayer from time to time.

Bible study groups which become mere talking shops only achieve half their purpose. In all these stories the women who met Jesus grew in their faith and went away as changed people. Mary Magdalene, for example, brought the good news that Jesus is alive to other people. Consider what you and your group can do towards understanding, enabling, and empowering women in the Church.

A PRAYER

Come to us, co-creating spirit of God,
and fill our hearts with love,
our minds with power,
our hands with skill;
that in unison with you
we women may be seen
to cherish and renew
the face of the earth
and live in joyful harmony
with all of creation. Amen

INTRODUCTION

Women make up half the human race and more than half the Christian Church! From the time of Jesus they have served the Christian community using "their own resources" (Luke 8.3). There have been women saints and martyrs, mystics and missionaries, preachers and pray-ers, nuns and nurses, and countless nameless women who have served the Church in the world in invisible and unsung ways.

Despite Jesus' own encouragement of women, the example of women like Hilda of Whitby or Teresa of Avila (both outstanding leaders of their times) and the unobtrusive witness of the Society of Friends and the Salvation Army, most of the Christian Church is only now beginning to consider the full contribution which women might make to its ministry and mission. For their part, women themselves are becoming more ready and willing to explore, value, and share their experiences to the benefit of all.

These Bible studies have been devised principally for groups of women, or women and men, as an introduction, to explore the roles that women play in the Church and in society. This is not to exclude men's groups (which might have a very interesting time) though they might have to adapt some of the questions!

We are all at different stages on our Christian journey, and some stories from the Bible speak to us more readily than others. The six themes have been quite deliberately chosen from the Gospels rather than from the Bible as a whole. This is because the stories of Jesus and his encounters with women had already become so highly valued by the early Church that they were incorporated into the Gospel when the Gospels came to be written down a generation or so after the death and resurrection of Jesus.

The preservation of these stories within the tradition of the early Church may suggest that women played a greater part in its life than has generally been recognized. More significantly, taken together the records show that Jesus' relationship with women, sometimes through quite brief encounters and sometimes as his companions and friends, forms an integral part of the good news of his coming, especially in a society where women were virtually excluded from public religious life.

The stories of these women often "ring bells" with the experiences of many women in the Church today. By facing issues which arise from these encounters with Jesus, and by opening up discussion in an atmosphere of mutual respect and understanding, it is hoped that women and men will grow in their love of God and will be both challenged and encouraged in their calling to be disciples of the risen Lord.

SESSION ONE

BEING, DOING, AND BELIEVING

[38]As Jesus and his disciples went on their way, he came to a village where a woman named Martha welcomed him in her home. [39]She had a sister named Mary, who sat down at the feet of the Lord and listened to his teaching. [40]Martha was upset over all the work she had to do, so she came and said, "Lord, don't you care that my sister has left me to do all the work by myself? Tell her to come and help me!"

[41]The Lord answered her, "Martha, Martha! You are worried and troubled over so many things, [42]but just one is needed. Mary has chosen the right thing, and it will not be taken away from her."

Luke 10.38–42

[17]When Jesus arrived, he found that Lazarus had been buried four days before. [18]Bethany was less than three kilometres from Jerusalem, [19]and many Judaeans had come to see Martha and Mary to comfort them over their brother's death.

[20]When Martha heard that Jesus was coming, she went out to meet him, but Mary stayed in the house. [21]Martha said to Jesus, "If you had been here, Lord, my brother would not have died! [22]But I know that even now God will give you whatever you ask him for."

[23]"Your brother will rise to life," Jesus told her.

[24]"I know," she replied, "that he will rise to life on the last day."

[25]Jesus said to her, "I am the resurrection and the life. Whoever believes in me will live, even though he dies; [26]and whoever lives and believes in me will never die. Do you believe this?"

[27]"Yes, Lord!" she answered. "I do believe that you are the Messiah, the Son of God, who was to come into the world."

John 11.17–27

In this session you will begin to think about women in the Church today, and how identifying with Martha or Mary challenges Christian traditions.

TO BEGIN

Divide into two groups, preferably men in one group, women in the other (it does not matter if the numbers are uneven). If you are an all-women group just divide into two sub-groups. On large sheets of paper, using felt pens, women make lists of the advantages and disadvantages of being a *man* in the Church, and men make lists of the advantages and disadvantages of being a *woman* in the Church. After a few minutes display your lists and compare them.

† What do the lists tell you about the expectations of women and men in the Church today?
† Do you want to add anything else to either list? If so, add it in a different colour.
† How do you feel about the lists now?

Ask the group leader to keep the papers until the final session.

Read Luke 10.38–42 aloud in the group.

DIGGING DEEPER

In the time of Jesus it was unheard of for a woman to sit at the feet of a rabbi or religious teacher, so Jesus was breaking with tradition in his encouragement of Mary.

In what ways do both Mary and Martha provide hospitality for Jesus? If you were Mary, what good points would you want to make in defence of Martha? If you were Martha how would you defend Mary? Does your Church regard its women members as "Marys" or "Marthas"?

How do you feel about this? What changes would you like to make? Why? How will you go about it?

Now read John 11.17–27.

In what ways do these verses, from the story of the raising of Lazarus from the dead, show a different side of Martha? Notice how she goes out to meet Jesus, trusts him, and shares her belief in life after death (verses 20–24).

Jesus replies with the last and greatest of his "I am" sayings in John's gospel (verse 25). What was he trying to convey to

Martha and his followers immediately before the raising of Lazarus and not long before his own death and resurrection? How would you explain the meaning and significance of this saying to a new Christian?

Martha's response (verse 27) is one of the most profound statements of faith in the Gospels. She sees Jesus as he really is, the Messiah, the Son of God. There is a sense in which for her Resurrection life has already begun.

TO TALK ABOUT

What connections do you see between "being, doing, and believing" in the light of these stories of Martha and Mary? Why do you think Jesus proclaimed "I am the resurrection and the life" to a woman in a community where women had little part in religious life? What does this reveal about Jesus' attitudes to women? Where do you see Jesus' attitudes reflected or ignored in your church?

Compare Martha's declaration here with Peter's confession of faith in Matthew 16.13–20. What has been the response of the Church to these respective statements? Has the Church managed to accept Jesus' attitudes to women throughout most of its history? How might women maintain or reclaim the tradition that Jesus himself initiated?

In what ways does your appreciation of Martha change when you take the stories in Luke and John together? How might they help you to value "Marthas" in the Church?

In the Middle Ages, whereas St George is said to have killed the dragon, there is another tradition which tells that Martha tamed the dragon and led it along. She is also shown preaching. How might these traditions affect your views of women in the Church today?

It is clear from the Gospels of Luke and John that women had a definite place in the life of the early Church. There are signs that more women are seeking a greater part in all aspects

9

of Church life today. Do you agree with this trend? Why or why not? How might the group act on its views?

TO PRAY

Thank God for all the "Marthas" and "Marys" in the Church today.

Pray for men and women who are trying to recover the early traditions of women in the Church, especially those who bear the pain of a restricted ministry.

Remember those who freely use their gifts serving the community.

Say the grace together.

SESSION TWO

AN UNLIKELY WITNESS

⁵In Samaria Jesus came to a town named Sychar, which was not far from the field that Jacob had given to his son Joseph. ⁶Jacob's well was there, and Jesus, tired out by the journey, sat down by the well. It was about noon.

⁷A Samaritan woman came to draw some water, and Jesus said to her, "Give me a drink of water." (⁸His disciples had gone into town to buy food.)

⁹The woman answered, "You are a Jew, and I am a Samaritan – so how can you ask me for a drink?" (Jews will not use the same cups and bowls that Samaritans use.)

¹⁰Jesus answered, "If only you knew what God gives and who it is that is asking you for a drink, you would ask him, and he would give you life-giving water."

¹¹"Sir," the woman said, "you haven't got a bucket, and the well is deep. Where would you get that life-giving water? ¹²It was our ancestor Jacob who gave us this well; he and his sons and his flocks all drank from it. You don't claim to be greater than Jacob, do you?"

¹³Jesus answered, "Whoever drinks this water will be thirsty again, ¹⁴but whoever drinks the water that I will give him will never be thirsty again. The water that I will give him will become in him a spring which will provide him with life-giving water and give him eternal life."

¹⁵"Sir," the woman said, "give me that water! Then I will never be thirsty again, nor will I have to come here to draw water."

¹⁶"Go and call your husband," Jesus told her, "and come back."

¹⁷"I haven't got a husband," she answered.

Jesus replied, "You are right when you say you haven't got a husband. ¹⁸You have been married to five men, and the man you live with now is not really your husband. You have told me the truth."

¹⁹"I see you are a prophet, sir," the woman said. ²⁰"My Samaritan ancestors worshipped God on this mountain, but you Jews say that Jerusalem is the place where we should worship God."

²¹Jesus said to her, "Believe me, woman, the time will come when people will not worship the Father either on this mountain or in Jerusalem. ²²You Samaritans do not really know whom you worship; but we Jews know whom we worship, because it is from the Jews that salvation comes. ²³But the time is coming and is already here, when by the power of God's Spirit people will worship the Father as he really is,

offering him the true worship that he wants. ²⁴God is Spirit, and only by the power of his Spirit can people worship him as he really is."

²⁵The woman said to him, "I know that the Messiah will come, and when he comes, he will tell us everything."

²⁶Jesus answered, "I am he, I who am talking with you."

²⁷At that moment Jesus' disciples returned, and they were greatly surprised to find him talking with a woman. But none of them said to her, "What do you want?" or asked him, "Why are you talking with her?"

²⁸Then the woman left her water jar, went back to the town, and said to the people there, ²⁹"Come and see the man who told me everything I have ever done. Could he be the Messiah?" ³⁰So they left the town and went to Jesus.

³⁹Many of the Samaritans in that town believed in Jesus because the woman had said, "He told me everything I have ever done." ⁴⁰So when the Samaritans came to him, they begged him to stay with them, and Jesus stayed there two days.

⁴¹Many more believed because of his message, ⁴²and they said to the woman, "We believe now, not because of what you said, but because we ourselves have heard him, and we know that he really is the Saviour of the world."

John 4.5–30, 39–42

In this session you will explore how Jesus makes himself known to the woman at the well, and how she changes from being alone and isolated to witnessing to the very people she was avoiding.

TO BEGIN

By yourself, think of an occasion when you felt really alone. Why was this? How did you cope? Talk about it as much as you wish with a partner. Remember to listen carefully to your partner and to keep faith with that trust.

Read John 4.5–30, 39–42.

DIGGING DEEPER

John sets the scene very carefully (verses 5–6). The Samaritans lived between Judaea and Galilee. Although they originally shared a common ancestry with the Jews they had different customs and, until its destruction, a rival temple on Mount Gerizim. In the time of Jesus bad feeling between Jews and Samaritans ran very high and they tried to avoid all contact.

As so often in John's gospel he describes what takes place and leaves his readers to work out what was really going on. For example, the mention of Jacob's well is highly significant and points not just to this particular meeting place but to the clash between the Jewish and Samaritan traditions. What clues does John give about the unnamed woman? Why was she at the well, by herself, at noon? How would she have been regarded by "religious" people, then and now?

"Listen in" to the three stages of the conversation:

Verses 7–15 How does Jesus make contact with the woman? What was so unusual about his request? Notice how the conversation develops on two levels, physical and spiritual. What did Jesus mean by "life-giving water"? What does water symbolize in both the Jewish and Christian traditions?

Verses 16–18 How and why does Jesus take the conversation further in verse 16? How does the woman react? What might she have been thinking?

Verses 19–26 Why does the woman try to change the subject in verse 19? What is new about the teaching of Jesus, and why does he choose to share it with a woman of dubious character, and a Samaritan too? How does she grow in her understanding of Jesus as the conversation takes its course?

Notice how Jesus reinterprets the Jewish tradition.

Jewish tradition	Jesus
Jacob's well	life-giving water for everyone
purification rules	asks for a drink from a *Samaritan woman*
water for man, and his flocks	living water for eternal life
worship in Jerusalem	worship in Spirit, truth
"Messiah will come"	"I am he"

13

Trace the woman's deepening knowledge of Jesus (verses 9, 12, 19, 29). What light does this throw on her character and needs? What immediate action does she take?

Why did Jesus choose such an unlikely woman to be a witness to him? In what ways did her witness compare with and differ from that of Andrew and Philip (John 1.40–42, 46–49)? How did the Samaritans respond? What new title did they give Jesus? What does this tell us about John's view of Jesus?

TO TALK ABOUT

The woman of Samaria was the first of many women who have been "unlikely witnesses" for Jesus. Many, such as Gladys Aylward, Amy Carmichael, Elizabeth Fry, and Mary Slessor, have made notable contributions to the world-wide Church. Who are their successors today?

What encouragement does this story offer to women in your Church? Do you ever think of yourself as an unlikely or unwilling witness or evangelist? How might the story of the Samaritan woman help you? What action will you take?

Why are there more women Church members than men?

Do women make better witnesses to the Christian faith than men?

What kind of welcome would your church give to a modern "woman of Samaria" who arrived on its doorstep? Be realistic!

Which of the titles of Jesus (Jew, prophet, Messiah, Saviour of the world, Lord) speaks to you today? What might any of these titles mean for people of other races and faiths, or of no faith? How might women and men together help those outside the Church to "believe now" that Jesus "really is the Saviour of the world" (verse 42)?

Jesus reinterpreted the Jewish tradition for his own time. In what ways are some women reinterpreting Christian traditions today? Do you support them? Why? Why not?

TO PRAY

In silence or aloud thank God for something you have learnt during this session.

Say together:

Almighty God,
in Christ you make all things new.
Transform the poverty of our nature
by the riches of your grace,
and in the renewal of our lives
make known your heavenly glory;
through Jesus Christ our Lord.

SESSION THREE

AN OUTSIDER

[21] Jesus left that place and went off to the territory near the cities of Tyre and Sidon. [22] A Canaanite woman who lived in that region came to him. "Son of David!" she cried out. "Have mercy on me, sir! My daughter has a demon and is in a terrible condition."

[23] But Jesus did not say a word to her. His disciples came to him and begged him, "Send her away! She is following us and making all this noise!"

[24] Then Jesus replied, "I have been sent only to the lost sheep of the people of Israel."

[25] At this the woman came and fell at his feet. "Help me, sir!" she said.

[26] Jesus answered, "It isn't right to take the children's food and throw it to the dogs."

[27] "That's true, sir," she answered; "but even the dogs eat the leftovers that fall from their masters' table."

[28] So Jesus answered her, "You are a woman of great faith! What you want will be done for you." And at that very moment her daughter was healed.

Matthew 15.21–28

In this session you will think about the encounter between the Canaanite woman and Jesus and his disciples, and how, through making herself vulnerable, she challenges Christians today to widen the boundaries of the Church, so that the Good News of Jesus is truly for everyone.

TO BEGIN

In pairs, discuss occasions when you have felt different or isolated from other people gathered around you, or when you felt shut out of a group. What did you want to do? Why? What did you do? Looking back now, would you act in the same way or differently in similar circumstances?
Read Matthew 15.21–28.

DIGGING DEEPER

Spend about half the time left "digging deeper".

Setting the scene. The Canaanite woman would have been regarded as a pagan by the Jews. She probably lived alone with her daughter (otherwise her husband would have approached Jesus on the daughter's behalf, as did Jairus). It was not customary for women to approach religious teachers at all, and certainly not on behalf of their daughters! Sons were much more highly valued. The woman would have known that Jesus would be regarded as ritually unclean as the result of her approach, and dogs in general had a bad name.

EITHER
a) Divide into two groups.

Group A
Imagine you are a Canaanite woman. Spend about five minutes by yourself reflecting:
What drives you to come to the Jewish teacher? How do you feel when you hear what the disciples are saying? What sort of help are you really expecting? Do you think Jesus is unwelcoming or is he teasing you? How do your feelings change? What change do you notice in Jesus? What do you want to say to Jesus when you realize your daughter has been healed?
Share your thoughts with the rest of your sub-group.

Group B
Imagine how Jesus felt. Spend five minutes by yourself reflecting on this episode in his life. Mark 7.24 suggests that he had left Judaea for some peace and quiet. How do you think he felt when the Canaanite woman arrived on the scene? What do you think he felt when he heard what the disciples were saying? Would they have reacted differently if the request had been made by a Jew, or for a son? What might

have been his immediate reaction to the woman's desperate cry for help on behalf of her daughter and herself? What might he be thinking as he replied to the woman? In what ways does the woman challenge his ministry?

Share your thoughts with the rest of your sub-group.

Together, as yourselves now, discuss in the whole group your thoughts and discoveries about this meeting between Jesus and the Canaanite woman.

OR
b) Discuss
In what ways did the woman make herself vulnerable when she came to Jesus? What risks did she take? Why did the disciples want to send her away? Do you find it easiest to identify with the woman, the disciples, or Jesus? Why is this? (You might find it helpful to reflect on some of the questions above.)

What did the woman learn from Jesus? What might the disciples have learned from both?

TO TALK ABOUT

In what ways, or on what occasions, do women today feel like "outsiders" in society and in the Church? Are there occasions when you feel an "outsider"? What do you do? Are there any times when vulnerability or weakness might help other people to understand the good news about Jesus?

Who are the "outsiders" in your local community? How do you relate to them, personally and in your local church? How easy is it for "outsiders" to join in your church services and church life? How might your church extend its "boundaries" to include them? What part might you play in this?

Below are various comments about this story. Spend a few minutes by yourself, arranging them in the order in which they appeal to you.
1. By her courage, faith, and insight the woman not only

gained wholeness and healing for her daughter, but gives new hope to all women who feel trapped by life's circumstances.

2. This story, of a woman challenging Jesus, suggests that women have a part to play today in widening the boundaries of Christian traditions.

3. Jesus had a sense of humour and was testing the woman's faith and teasing her so that she might share her lively wit.

4. By making herself vulnerable in coming to Jesus, and by her lively encounter and argument with him, the woman demonstrates the possibility of equality for men and women in the Church.

5. The Good News of Jesus is for everyone regardless of race, colour, social class, or creed: there are no "outsiders" in the kingdom of God.

Which comments are most important to the group as a whole? How does this reflect what the group feels about the place of women in the Church today? What action does the group need to take?

TO PRAY

Thank God for the gift of wholeness and healing through Jesus Christ, and commend to him those women and men who seek wholeness for others or for themselves.

Name, either silently or aloud, those who feel they are outsiders in society or Church, and those who work to include them.

Pray that you may have the will to respond to new thoughts and challenges which have come through the work of the group.

SESSION FOUR

A FEMININE PROPHET?

¹It was now two days before the Festival of Passover and Unleavened Bread. The chief priests and the teachers of the Law were looking for a way to arrest Jesus secretly and put him to death. ²"We must not do it during the festival," they said, "or the people might riot."

³Jesus was in Bethany at the house of Simon, a man who had suffered from a dreaded skin-disease. While Jesus was eating, a woman came in with an alabaster jar full of a very expensive perfume made of pure nard. She broke the jar and poured the perfume on Jesus' head. ⁴Some of the people there became angry and said to one another, "What was the use of wasting the perfume? ⁵It could have been sold for more than three hundred silver coins and the money given to the poor!" And they criticized her harshly.

⁶But Jesus said, "Leave her alone! Why are you bothering her? She has done a fine and beautiful thing for me. ⁷You will always have poor people with you, and any time you want to, you can help them. But you will not always have me. ⁸She did what she could; she poured perfume on my body to prepare it ahead of time for burial. ⁹Now, I assure you that wherever the gospel is preached all over the world, what she has done will be told in memory of her."

¹⁰Then Judas Iscariot, one of the twelve disciples, went off to the chief priests in order to betray Jesus to them. ¹¹They were pleased to hear what he had to say, and promised to give him money. So Judas started looking for a good chance to hand Jesus over to them.

Mark 14.1–11

In this session you will explore the story of the anointing of Jesus at Bethany, and how it might challenge our assumptions, traditions, and values.

TO BEGIN

Collect a variety of women's magazines and Church newspapers (any denomination). What do they suggest are the main interests of women? Many women's magazines feature various needs of the body; health and beauty, food, fashion, sexuality, and human relationships. At what points do the magazine features and the Church press relate (or fail to relate) to your own experience as women, and as women in the Church?

Read Mark 14.1–11

DIGGING DEEPER

What was happening in Jerusalem? Verses 1–2 set the scene for this story. Why was this a crucial time for Jesus?

At table Jesus was reclining with others at a low table, resting on his left elbow. The tables were usually arranged around three sides of a square to allow the servants to wait on the (male) guests. It was often easy to gatecrash a party.

Alabaster was a creamy white gypsum resembling marble, often used for small jars of expensive perfume.

Nard or spikenard: a plant from which a fragrant perfume was made. Imported from India it was a great luxury. The jar cost the equivalent of a labourer's annual wage. To break the jar and use it all at once was most extravagant!

Anointing was common in the time of Jesus when the head or person of a guest was often anointed with a few drops of perfume or olive oil (Luke 7.46). The sick were anointed (Mark 6.13), as were the dead (Luke 23.56), when the fragments of the broken jar were sometimes buried with the body. According to Jewish tradition, priests (Exodus 28.41), prophets (1 Kings 19.16) and kings (1 Samuel 10.1, and 2 Samuel 2.4) were all anointed – by men. The Hebrew word "Messiah" (Greek, "Christ"), meaning "the anointed one", was the title given by the prophets to the Saviour promised by God.

Look again at verses 1–2 and 10–11. What made the woman's action prophetic at this stage of Jesus' life? What traditions and values are being re-shaped in this story?

What is Mark telling his readers about Jesus? Divide into

21

three groups representing the woman, the people, and Jesus respectively. Spend a few minutes thinking about what happened. What do you know about the person or people you represent? What words would you use to describe the woman's act of love? What do you think and feel about it? How would you describe the reactions of the other people present?

Jesus makes four statements in verses 6–9. What does each say about Jesus and his attitudes to the woman and the other guests? What do you want to say to the other two groups?

Come together and say it!

Now as yourselves work out what assumptions you were making in your part and for the others who were present at the meal.

How did you justify your own actions or reactions?

TO TALK ABOUT

This impulsive woman poured out her love for Jesus in an extravagant gesture, and Jesus, far from being embarrassed, praised her for it. Do you think the Church today is afraid of "body language" in men and women? Talk about some examples for and against your views.

It is clear from verses 6–8 that Jesus not only accepts and fully appreciates the woman's action as a compassionate act of love; he also interprets it as a prophetic action. By acting in a prophetic, male role the woman reshapes the inherited tradition of the Jewish community, and is commended by Jesus for doing so. Are there any inherited traditions and values in the Church today which need reshaping? What are they? How might women (and men) help this process? What will you do?

Looking back to 1989 from, say, 2089, people may say that the consecration of the first woman bishop in the Anglican Communion (a black divorcee) was a prophetic act. How do you react to this suggestion in the light of the story of the woman who anointed Jesus? Are there feminine prophets in the contemporary Church?

Do you think women in the Church get the press they deserve? What will you do about it?

TO PRAY

Christ Jesus,
whose glory was poured out like perfume,
and who chose for our sake
to take the form of a slave:
may we also pour out our love
with holy extravagance,
that our lives may be fragrant with you.
Amen

SESSION FIVE

AN APOSTLE TO THE APOSTLES

[1]*Some time later Jesus travelled through towns and villages, preaching the Good News about the Kingdom of God. The twelve disciples went with him,* [2]*and so did some women who had been healed of evil spirits and diseases: Mary (who was called Magdalene), from whom seven demons had been driven out;* [3]*Joanna, whose husband Chuza was an officer in Herod's court; and Susanna, and many other women who used their own resources to help Jesus and his disciples.*

Luke 8.1–3

[1]*Early on Sunday morning, while it was still dark, Mary Magdalene went to the tomb and saw that the stone had been taken away from the entrance.* [2]*She went running to Simon Peter and the other disciple, whom Jesus loved, and told them, "They have taken the Lord from the tomb, and we don't know where they have put him!"* [11]*Mary stood crying outside the tomb. While she was still crying, she bent over and looked in the tomb* [12]*and saw two angels there dressed in white, sitting where the body of Jesus had been, one at the head and the other at the feet.* [13]*"Woman, why are you crying?" they asked her.*

She answered, "They have taken my Lord away, and I do not know where they have put him!"

[14]*Then she turned round and saw Jesus standing there; but she did not know that it was Jesus.* [15]*"Woman, why are you crying?" Jesus asked her, "Who is it that you are looking for?"*

She thought he was the gardener, so she said to him, "If you took him away, sir, tell me where you have put him, and I will go and get him."

[16]*Jesus said to her, "Mary!"*

She turned towards him and said in Hebrew, "Rabboni!" (This means "Teacher.")

[17]*"Do not hold on to me," Jesus told her, "because I have not yet gone back up to the Father. But go to my brothers and tell them that I am returning to him who is my Father and their Father, my God and their God."*

[18]*So Mary Magdalene went and told the disciples that she had seen the Lord and related to them what he had told her.*

John 20.1–2, 11–18

In this session you will focus on the story of Mary Magdalene whom Jesus chose to be the first messenger of the resurrection, and see that the resurrection faith has to be shared with others.

TO BEGIN

By yourselves, make a list of ten well-known Christian women, living or dead. By the side of each name write one thing for which they are famous. Compare your lists in the group. What similarities or differences do you notice?

Read Luke 8.1–3 and John 20.1–2, 11–18.

DIGGING DEEPER

Mary Magdalene has had a bad press! In the Church's tradition she has been confused with prostitutes and "fallen women". What does Luke 8.1–3 tell you about her? Look up Mark 15.40–41. In what way does Mark confirm what Luke writes? What do the two passages suggest about Mary's relationship with Jesus? All the Gospels name her as one of the women who followed Jesus to the cross.

Mary had experienced healing and wholeness of body, mind, and spirit through Jesus. As one of the closest woman followers of Jesus, who had supported him with her wealth and stayed with him throughout his suffering on the cross, her grief must have been overwhelming. In her meeting with Jesus on the first Easter morning she had to face up to the conflict deep within herself between holding on to the past and being open to the future (verse 17). Why do you think Jesus chose her to be his apostle to the apostles?

The following section may be approached in three ways:
1. With the group members imagining they are standing in the shoes of Mary Magdalene and going through the section reflecting on the questions, etc. This is not an easy exercise, but many groups find it very profitable. It can, of course, be done by individuals or with a friend at home.

25

2. As a general group discussion with everyone pooling their ideas.

3. As a meditation, with the leader or another group member (after preparation and some adaptation) reading through the passage slowly, allowing a period for silent reflection as appropriate, and possibly a space for general discussion at the end.

By yourselves imagine you are Mary standing in the garden on the first Easter morning. You were up very early, and shocked to discover the empty tomb (John 20.1–2). Now you have come back again. Why? What are you thinking as you stand crying by the tomb?

Read through the passage again, and listen again as Jesus speaks to you (verses 15, 16, and 17). How do your feelings change as Jesus speaks? What happens when he calls you by your own name? Why does he tell you not to hold on to him? How has he changed? How does he help you to accept the grief of parting? What task does he entrust to you? What do you think his message means? How do you feel as you undertake the task?

You are convinced you "have seen the Lord". What if the disciples don't believe you (see Luke 24.11)?

Share your thoughts with a partner. Then discuss things together with the whole group as appropriate.

Now go over the story again as yourself. What sorrows do you need to name before Jesus? Do you hear Jesus calling you by your own name? How important is that to you? Why is it out of place to cling on to Jesus? What do you want to say to him?

Jesus has a task for you too; "Go . . . and tell . . .". What does that mean to you in your life? What is Jesus asking you to do now? How will you respond? Do you share Mary's joy?

Discuss your thoughts with your partner in turn. Listen carefully to your partner and try not to interrupt. What support will you give?

26

TO TALK ABOUT

"I have seen the Lord." How real is your faith in the resurrection? What difference does it make to your life? How do you share or proclaim your faith in the Risen Lord? What helps you most? What hinders you? What steps can you take to overcome the hindrances? Who can help you?

In the past many women went abroad as missionaries as there was little scope for full-time service in the Church at home. What do you think Mary Magdalene might want to say to women in the Church today? What might she want to say to men?

Go back to the lists you made at the beginning of this session. What range of gifts do or did these women bring to the Christian community? Why is the Church today so slow to recognize the God-given gifts and potential of more than half of its members?

Jesus clearly gave Mary Magdalene a position of responsibility at the time of his resurrection. Do you think that women should become Church leaders? The Society of Friends (Quakers) and the Salvation Army have always thought so. Who are the women leaders in your Church? What qualities do they need? Should the Church recreate a tradition of leadership by women and men? If so, what action needs to be taken by women now, and by men? What action will the group take?

TO PRAY

In silence, bring to God one thing you have learnt during this session, and pray for one another and for all women Church leaders.

Living God, who came to your world and entered human pain
– Come and be in every painful place in our lives, in every painful
  place in our world, today.
Living God, who worked in the secret darkness to raise Christ
  from the grave

27

*– Come and work in every secret, dark place of our lives, in every
secret, dark place of our world, today.*
*Living God, who sent women out to proclaim the resurrection to
the frightened, imprisoned disciples,*
*– Come and empower us in every frightened, imprisoned place in
our lives, in every frightened, imprisoned place in our world
today.*
Living God, Risen God, Easter God:
– Come and make us your living Church,
                        your risen Church,
                        your Easter Church,
                        Today and every day.

or

Say together:

*"O God, the power of the powerless,
you have chosen as your witnesses
those whose voice is not heard.
Grant that, as women first
announced the resurrection
though they were not believed,
we too may have courage
to persist in proclaiming your Word,
in the power of Jesus Christ.
Amen"*

SESSION SIX

A SWORD IN THE HEART OF MARY

[26] *In the sixth month of Elizabeth's pregnancy God sent the angel Gabriel to a town in Galilee named Nazareth.* [27] *He had a message for a girl promised in marriage to a man named Joseph, who was a descendant of King David. The girl's name was Mary.* [28] *The angel came to her and said, "Peace be with you! The Lord is with you and has greatly blessed you!"*

[29] *Mary was deeply troubled by the angel's message, and she wondered what his words meant.* [30] *The angel said to her, "Don't be afraid, Mary; God has been gracious to you.* [31] *You will become pregnant and give birth to a son, and you will name him Jesus.* [32] *He will be great and will be called the Son of the Most High God. The Lord God will make him a king, as his ancestor David was,* [33] *and he will be the king of the descendants of Jacob for ever; his kingdom will never end!"*

[34] *Mary said to the angel, "I am a virgin. How, then, can this be?"*

[35] *The angel answered, "The Holy Spirit will come on you, and God's power will rest upon you. For this reason the holy child will be called the Son of God.* [36] *Remember your relative Elizabeth. It is said that she cannot have children, but she herself* is now six months pregnant, even though she is very old.* [37] *For there is nothing that God cannot do."*

[38] *"I am the Lord's servant," said Mary; "may it happen to me as you have said." And the angel left her.*
Luke 1.26–38

[1] *At that time the Emperor Augustus ordered a census to be taken throughout the Roman Empire.* [2] *When this first census took place, Quirinius was the governor of Syria.* [3] *Everyone, then, went to register himself, each to his own town.*

[4] *Joseph went from the town of Nazareth in Galilee to the town of Bethlehem in Judaea, the birthplace of King David. Joseph went there because he was a descendant of David.* [5] *He went to register with Mary, who was promised in marriage to him. She was pregnant,* [6] *and while they were in Bethlehem, the time came for her to have her baby.* [7] *She gave birth to her first son, wrapped him in strips of cloth and laid him in a manger – there was no room for them to stay in the inn.*

[Shepherds saw an army of angels and said,] "Let's go to Bethlehem and see this thing that has happened, which the Lord has told us."

[16] *So they hurried off and found*

29

Mary and Joseph and saw the baby lying in the manger. [17]When the shepherds saw him, they told them what the angel had said about the child. [18]All who heard it were amazed at what the shepherds said. [19]Mary remembered all these things and thought deeply about them.

[22]The time came for Joseph and Mary to perform the ceremony of purification, as the Law of Moses commanded.

[25]At that time there was a man named Simeon living in Jerusalem ... [27]Led by the Spirit, Simeon went into the Temple ... [28]Simeon took the child in his arms and gave thanks to God:

[29]"Now, Lord, you have kept your promise,
and you may let your servant go in peace.

[30]With my own eyes I have seen your salvation,
[31] which you have prepared in the presence of all peoples:
[32]A light to reveal your will to the Gentiles
and bring glory to your people Israel."

[34]Simeon blessed them and said to Mary, his mother, "This child is chosen by God for the destruction and the salvation of many in Israel. He will be a sign from God which many people will speak against [35]and so reveal their secret thoughts. And sorrow, like a sharp sword, will break your own heart."
Luke 2.1–7, 15–19, 22, 25, 27, 28– 32, 34–35

In this session you will begin with the birth of Jesus and look at some of the Gospel records of Mary, the mother of Jesus, and how they helped to form the tradition of the Church. You will also consider ways in which women in the Church today might carry the tradition forward.

TO BEGIN

By yourself make a list of thoughts which come into your mind when you hear or see the words "Virgin Mary" or "Mary the mother of Jesus". Allow just two or three minutes. On a large sheet of paper write up the different thoughts represented in the group. How does the list reflect the place of Mary in the life and tradition of the Church, past and present?
Read Luke 1.26–38; 2.1–35.

DIGGING DEEPER

The birth of Jesus

Go through the readings again and note down what they tell you about Jesus and about Mary. If your time is limited do this in two groups.

What expectations about Jesus and Mary does Luke arouse for the rest of his Gospel? Compare Matthew 1.18 24. What does he add to Luke's account?

However you understand these verses, the main point is that they show Mary consenting of her own free will to co-operate with God's plan for the world. Suppose the first two chapters of Luke had been lost. What difference would that have made to the Christian tradition concerning Mary?

What do you think Simeon meant in verse 35? What might the words have meant to Mary at the time, and looking back after the resurrection?

Mary in the Gospels

Look up Mark 3.20–21, 31–33; 6.2–3; John 2.1–12; 19.25–27; Acts 1.12–14.

Why do you think there is so little about Mary in the Gospels? Mary's presence at the cross is only mentioned in John's gospel and Acts 1.14 is the only time Mary is mentioned outside the Gospels. What do these passages suggest about the relationship between Jesus and his mother? Why do you think being the mother of Jesus might have been a bewildering experience for Mary? In what ways was Simeon's prophecy fulfilled?

How might the experiences of mothers today resemble or differ from those of Mary? In what ways has the Church's honouring of Mary and rejection of Eve made life easier or more difficult for women in and out of church?

TO TALK ABOUT

Bearing in mind that nowhere in the New Testament is belief in the virgin birth explicitly required faith for a Christian, how would you respond to someone unable to accept the phrase "Born of the Virgin Mary"?

Go through the list you made at the beginning of the session. Mark with a *B* any ideas which have a direct connection with the Bible. Then mark with a *C* those which belong to the tradition of the Church. Don't worry if some have both letters and some neither! What conclusions about the Church's tradition concerning Mary do you want to draw from the list? Do you want to change that tradition in any way? If so, how would you change it, and why?

It has been said that Mary Magdalene, because she was faithful at the cross (recorded in all the Gospels) and because Jesus entrusted to her the message of the resurrection, is more representative of the role of women in the Church today than Mary the mother of Jesus. Do you agree? Why? Why not?

In previous sessions we have thought about *Being*, *Doing*, and *Believing* and Jesus' encouragement of both Martha and Mary; the woman of Samaria as *An Unlikely Witness*; the Canaanite *Outsider* who in her vulnerability and her wit challenged Jesus; *A Feminine Prophet* who in one extravagant, compassionate gesture anointed Jesus "for burial"; and Mary Magdalene, sent as *An Apostle to the Apostles*. We have seen how Jesus accepted the very varied ministry of these women. Why do you think some Churches today restrict their women's ministry?

Jesus helped women, and his followers and opponents, to question in different ways the traditions of a community which denied women a place in its public religious life. In what ways might Jesus be encouraging the members of your group to question traditions of the Church today and reshape them for the future? How will you proceed if you cannot agree?

If you can, look again at the lists you made at the first session on the advantages and disadvantages of being women and men in the Church today. In what ways have your thoughts and feelings changed as a result of these studies? Have there been any times when you have felt upset, or particularly reassured or challenged? Why was this? How do you feel now? What do you want to say to the men in your local church? What do you want to say to your Church leaders, locally and nationally?

What action will you take, individually and as a group, as a result of these studies? How might women and men work together as partners for the kingdom of God, appreciating and valuing one another's varied gifts and skills?

TO PRAY
In thanksgiving, love, and hope say together Mary's Song:

My heart praises the Lord;
  my soul is glad because of God my Saviour,
  for he has remembered me, his lowly servant!
From now on all people will call me happy,
  because of the great things the Mighty God has done for me.
His name is holy;
  from one generation to another
  he shows mercy to those who honour him.
He has stretched out his mighty arm
  and scattered the proud with all their plans.
He has brought down mighty kings from their thrones,
  and lifted up the lowly.
He has filled the hungry with good things,
  and sent the rich away with empty hands.
He has kept the promise he made to our ancestors,
  and has come to the help of his servant Israel.
He has remembered to show mercy to Abraham
  and to all his descendants for ever!

Join hands and say the grace together.